Worn Red Theatre and Ben Canni
in association with Clean Break a
for the Finborough Theatre
presents

The World Premiere

WITHDRAWN

And I and Silence

by Naomi Wallace

WORN RED THEATRE   **CLEAN BREAK**

FINBOROUGH | THEATRE

And I and Silence was originally commissioned by Clean Break.
And I and Silence originally received a staged reading at the
Finborough Theatre as part of *Vibrant – An Anniversary Festival
of Finborough Playwrights*: Friday 18 June 2010
                                              borough Theatre: Tuesday 10 May 2011

Foreword

Lucy Morrison, *Head of Artistic Programme, Clean Break*

And I and Silence was originally commissioned by Clean Break. As part of the process Naomi Wallace and I ran a series of playwriting workshops in HMP Morton Hall in 2008, where at the time, the majority of the women imprisoned were from overseas. For many, whose overriding experience of Britain was with the criminal justice system and subsequently incarceration, there was, not surprisingly, a strong sense of displacement. Yet the women, whose crimes were largely motivated by poverty, shared so much. It became clear over the weeks that the workshops provided vital space for what felt, at times, to be an overwhelming need for the women to tell stories and connect with one another. *And I and Silence* gives powerful expression to the sheer force of love that women, who have nothing and nowhere, are capable of.

And I and Silence

by Naomi Wallace

Cast in alphabetical order

Young Dee	**Lauren Crace**
Dee	**Sally Oliver**
Jamie	**Cat Simmons**
Young Jamie	**Cherrelle Skeete**

1950 and 1959. Past and Present. Somewhere in the USA.

Director	**Caitlin McLeod**
Set Designer	**Cecilia Carey**
Lighting Designer	**Elliot Griggs**
Costume Designer	**Ed Parry**
Music	**Ben Osborn** and **Tegid Cartwright**
Assistant Director	**Tim Newns**

Production Acknowledgements

Company Stage Manager | **Hannah Gore**
Assistant Set Designer | **Bethany Sumner**
Lighting Operator | **Bethany Sumner**
Fight Director | **Kevin McCurdy**
Press Representative | **Finborough Theatre** 07977 173135

The playwright would like to give special thanks to Lucy Morrison from Clean Break for her invaluable work with the initial writing of *And I and Silence*.

The performance lasts approximately 75 minutes.
There will be no interval.

Our patrons are respectfully reminded that, in this intimate theatre, any noise such as rustling programmes, talking or the ringing of mobile phones may distract the actors and your fellow audience-members.

Lauren Crace | Young Dee

At the Finborough Theatre, Lauren played Young Dee in *And I and Silence* as part of *Vibrant – An Anniversary Festival of Finborough Playwrights* (2010).

Trained at the Royal Academy of Dramatic Art.

Theatre includes *Les Liaisons Dangereuses* (Salisbury Playhouse).

TV includes *Holby City* (BBC), *Room at the Top* (BBC), *Silk* (BBC), *Sherlock – The Great Game* (BBC) and *EastEnders* (BBC) for which she was awarded 'Best Newcomer' at the TV Quick/ TV Choice Awards 2009.

Audio Drama includes *The Minister Of Chance* (Radiostatic).

Rehearsed readings include *Skyvers* (National Theatre) and *Spur of The Moment* (Royal Court Theatre).

Sally Oliver | Dee

Trained at the Webber Douglas Academy of Dramatic Art.

Theatre includes *Two Women* (Theatre Royal Stratford East), *Cinderella* (Hexagon Theatre), *Proof* (Arts Theatre, London, and Birmingham Stage Company) and *Charley's Aunt* (Southwold Summer Theatre).

TV and Film includes *Holby City* (BBC), *Emmerdale* (Yorkshire Television) and *Come Rain Come Shine* (ITV).

Cat Simmons | Jamie

Theatre includes *Coming Home* (Arcola Theatre), *Been So Long* (The Young Vic and English Touring Theatre), *America Visions of Love* (Winter Guests), *We Happy Few* (Gielgud Theatre), *Simply Heavenly* (The Young Vic and National Theatre Studio), *Aladdin* (The Old Vic), *Fame* (Cambridge Theatre), *Jesus Christ Superstar* (National Tour for The Really Useful Group) and *Whistle Down The Wind* (Aldwych Theatre).

TV and Radio includes *Casualty* (BBC), *The Bill* (Talkback Thames), *Doctors* (BBC), *Family Affairs* (Talkback Thames), *No Angels* (World Productions), *Girl's Weekend* (BBC) *Factory Children* and *Hanging of Ernest Moon* (BBC Drama).

Film includes *Life and Lyrics* (Fiesta Production) and *Postcode* (Ladysmith Productions).

Cherrelle Skeete | Young Jamie

Trained at the Central School of Speech and Drama.

Theatre includes *The Edge* (New Diorama Theatre), *SOLD* and *King Lear* (Central School of Speech and Drama).

Rehearsed readings include *Not Quite Gospel* (Nu Century Arts) and *A Teenagers Guide to Surviving Sex Slavery* from *I am an Emotional Creature* (WOW Festival).

Naomi Wallace | Playwright

Naomi's first play, *The War Boys*, was produced at the Finborough Theatre in 1993. Her work has been produced in the United Kingdom, Europe, the Middle East and the United States. Her major plays include *One Flea Spare*, *In the Heart of America*, *Slaughter City*, *The Trestle at Pope Lick Creek*, *Things of Dry Hours* and *The Fever Chart: Three Short Visions of the Middle East*. Among other awards, her work has twice received the Susan Smith Blackburn Prize, and an Obie. She is also a recipient of the MacArthur "Genius" Fellowship. *And I and Silence* received a reading in last year's *Vibrant – An Anniversary Festival of Finborough Playwrights*.

Caitlin McLeod | Director

At the Finborough Theatre, Caitlin directed the Great Britain premiere of Stewart Parker's *Northern Star* (2011) and a staged reading of *And I and Silence* as part of *Vibrant – An Anniversary Festival of Finborough Playwrights* (2010).

Directing includes the *One Short Sleepe* (South Bank Literary Festival), *Seven Jewish Children* (The Capital Centre), *The Lady's Not For Burning* and the UK Premiere of *Elephant's Graveyard* (Warwick Arts Centre) which went on to win four awards at the National Student Drama Festival including the Buzz Goodbody Award for Best Director. Assistant Direction includes *Hamlet* (Shakespeare's Globe Tour), *The Talented Mr Ripley* (Royal and Derngate Theatres, Northampton) and *Touched* (North Wall Theatre, Oxford and Latitude Festival).

Cecilia Carey | Set Designer

Trained at Motley Theatre Design Course. Theatre includes *The Red Helicopter* (Almeida Theatre), *Puss in Boots* (Derby Guildhall for Derby Live), *Scarlet's Circus* (Hampstead Theatre) and *Anemone* (Sprint Festival at Camden People's Theatre). Site specific work includes *The Great Train Dance* (Severn Valley Railway), *Architectural Punchbowl* (Bompas and Parr) and *Indiana Jones Taste-O-Rama* (Harley Gallery, Welbeck Abbey). Cecilia has also assisted on *Lucrezia Borgia* (English National Opera), *Batman Arena World Tour*, concerts for Kanye West and Lady Gaga and the *Progress Tour* for Take That.

Elliot Griggs | Lighting Designer

At the Finborough Theatre, Elliot was Lighting Designer for *Northern Star* (2011).

Other lighting designs include *The Lady's Not For Burning* (Warwick Arts Centre), *Drift: Photo 51* (Curious Directive at the Edinburgh Academy), *West Side Story* (Warwick Arts Centre), *The Mercy Seat* (Capital Centre), *By The Bog of Cats*, *'Tis Pity She's a Whore*, *Elephant's Graveyard* (Warwick Arts Centre), *Much Ado About Nothing* (Belgrade Theatre), *Dido and Aeneas* (St. Paul's Church and Tour) and *Gutted: The Revenger's Musical* (Riverside Studios). Assistant designs includes *The Young Idea* (Royal Academy of Dramatic Art) and *Blavatsky's Tower* (Camden People's Theatre). He was awarded the ShowLight Award for Lighting Design at the National Student Drama Festival in 2009.

Ed Parry | Costume Designer

Trained at Aberystwyth University, graduating with a First Class BA Hons in Scenography and Theatre Design in 2009, and receiving the highest Single Honours result in the Faculty of Arts. Theatre includes Assistant Costume Supervisor for *Sister Act* (National UK Tour and Vienna), Costume Supervisor for *Precious Little Talent* (Trafalgar Studios), Assistant Costume Supervisor for *Wicked* (Apollo Victoria Theatre), Costume Supervisor for *Platform* (Old Vic Tunnels), Costume Supervisor for *Bud Take The Wheel I Feel A Song Coming On* (Edinburgh Festival), Assistant Costume Supervisor for *The Railway Children* (Waterloo Station), and Costume Daily for *A Tale of Two Cities* (Theatre Royal Brighton).

Ben Osborn | Music

At the Finborough Theatre, Ben was Co-Musical Director and Composer for *Northern Star* (2011).

Other theatre includes *Sum* (Clayesmore School), *No Wonder* (Library Theatre, Manchester), *The Wind in the Willows* (Theatre503) and *Touched* (Latitude Festival). His soundtrack to *By the Bog of Cats* (National Student Drama Festival) won the Cameron Mackintosh Award in 2010. He is also a songwriter, and performs in various bands.

Tegid Cartwright | Music

At the Finborough Theatre, Tegid was Co-Musical Director and Composer for *Northern Star* (2011).

Tegid has composed music for a theatrical adaptation of Sylvain Chomet's animation *Belleville Rendez-Vous* and has worked as a creative director and dramaturg on a number of projects including a dance piece *Remember When* (Nottingham Playhouse), *By The Bog Of Cats* (Warwick Arts Centre) and Christopher Fry's *The Lady's Not For Burning* (Warwick Arts Centre). Tegid collaborates with various companies, in addition to Worn Red Theatre, including The Nomad Projeckt and FellSwoop Theatre Company.

Tim Newns | Assistant Director

At the Finborough Theatre, Tim directed Harold Brighouse's *The Northerners* (2010) and was Resident Assistant Director during 2009 where he assisted on *The Druid's Rest* (2009), *I Was A Beautiful Day* (2009), *Country Magic* (2009) and *And I and Silence* as part of *Vibrant – An Anniversary Festival of Finborough Playwrights* (2010). He also produced *Country Magic* and *The Druid's Rest*.

Directing includes *Angeldust* (Etcetera Theatre). Assistant Direction includes *Much* (Cock Tavern) and *Julius Caesar* (Liverpool Everyman and Playhouse Youth Theatre). He is Artistic Director of Chequered Blue Theatre.

Rachel Payant | Casting Director

Rachel is Casting Associate at the Finborough Theatre. Castings for the Finborough Theatre include *Love Child* (2006) *Little Madam* (2007), *Sons of York* (2008), *Captain Oates Left Sock* (2009),*Dream of the Dog* and its subsequent transfer to Trafalgar Studios (2010) and *The December Man/L'homme de decembre* (2011).

Television assisting work includes *Masterwork* (Fox) and *The Freaky Farleys* (RDF and Nickelodeon).

Worn Red Theatre | Producer

Worn Red Theatre champion playwrights and subjects rarely explored in the mainstream. Through challenging their audiences and stirring debate, Worn Red creates theatre that extends beyond the walls of the auditorium. Their most recent production was *Northern Star* by Stewart Parker, part of the RediscoveriesUK season at the Finborough Theatre. Never before performed in Great Britain, *Northern Star* was named *Time Out* Critics' Choice.

Ben Canning | Producer

Past productions include *Boy in Darkness* by Tim Franklin and Liz Sands (Edinburgh Festival), *Elephant's Graveyard* by George Brant (National Student Drama Festival), *100* by TheImaginaryBody (Northern Ireland Tour), '*Tis Pity She's A Whore* by John Ford (Warwick Arts Centre), *Wonderland* (Warwick Arts Centre), *Bottom of the Pit* (site-specific), *A Passage to India* by Santha Rama Rau (Capital Centre, Coventry). As co-founder and producer for theatre company curious directive (www.curiousdirective.com), productions include *Le Corps Perdue, Drift*, *Photo 51* and *Snow Base: Triptych* (Edinburgh Academy for the Edinburgh International Science Festival) and *Return to the Silence* (Pleasance London). In 2010, he coordinated Europe's largest student-run arts festival (WSAF), programming over one hundred theatre, dance, art, performance, literature and music events. He was also the Windsor Festival Theatre Coordinator in 2009 and 2010.

Lydia Rynne | Associate Producer

At the Finborough Theatre, Lydia was Producer for Worn Red Theatre's production of *Northern Star* (2011).

She is one of the founders of FellSwoop Theatre Company (http://fellswooptheatre.wordpress.com/) and was a Creative Producer for *Most Drink in Secret* (The Spring, Havant, and Tobacco Factory, Bristol) and the world premiere stage adaptation of Sylvain Chomet's animation film *Belleville Rendez-vous* (Bedlam Theatre, Edinburgh Festival 2011). Lydia was on the executive production team behind *One World Week 2009* and *Warwick Student Arts Festival 2010* – two of the largest student-run arts/culture festivals in the UK. She also helped produce *Faith, Hope and Charity* (LEAP Productions at Southwark Playhouse) and is an active member of the science theatre company Curious Directive as a deviser/performer.

Clean Break | Associate Producer

Clean Break is a producing theatre company with an independent education programme. Both strands of our work are rooted in the belief that theatre changes lives. Behind the scenes, we provide high-quality theatre-based courses, qualifications, training opportunities and specialist support which are critical for the rehabilitation of women offenders. On the stage, we produce ground-breaking and award winning plays which dramatise women's experience of, and relationship to, crime and punishment.

www.cleanbreak.org.uk
www.facebook.com/cleanbreak
www.twitter.com/CleanBrk

FINBOROUGH | THEATRE

Winner – *London Theatre Reviews'* Empty Space Peter Brook Award 2010

"One of the most stimulating venues in London, fielding a programme that is a bold mix of trenchant, politically thought-provoking new drama and shrewdly chosen revivals of neglected works from the past." *The Independent*

"A disproportionately valuable component of the London theatre ecology. Its programme combines new writing and revivals, in selections intelligent and audacious." *Financial Times*

"A blazing beacon of intelligent endeavour, nurturing new writers while finding and reviving neglected curiosities from home and abroad." *The Daily Telegraph*

Founded in 1980, the multi-award-winning Finborough Theatre presents plays and music theatre, concentrated exclusively on new writing and rediscoveries from the 19th and 20th centuries. We offer a stimulating and inclusive programme, appealing to theatregoers of all generations and from a broad spectrum of the population. Behind the scenes, we continue to discover and develop a new generation of theatre makers – through our vibrant Literary Department, our internship programme, our Resident Assistant Director Programme, and our partnership with the National Theatre Studio – the Leverhulme Bursary for Emerging Directors.

Despite remaining completely unfunded, the Finborough Theatre has an unparalleled track record of attracting the finest creative talent to work with us, as well as discovering new playwrights who go on to become leading voices in British theatre. Under Artistic Director Neil McPherson, it has discovered some of the UK's most exciting new playwrights including Laura Wade, James Graham, Mike Bartlett, Sarah Grochala, Jack Thorne, Simon Vinnicombe, Alexandra Wood, Al Smith, Nicholas de Jongh and Anders Lustgarten.

Artists working at the theatre in the 1980s included Clive Barker, Rory Bremner, Nica Burns, Kathy Burke, Ken Campbell, Jane Horrocks and Claire Dowie. In the 1990s, the Finborough Theatre became known for new writing including Naomi Wallace's first play *The War Boys*; Rachel Weisz in David Farr's *Neville Southall's Washbag*; four plays by Anthony Neilson including *Penetrator* and *The Censor*, both of which transferred to the Royal Court Theatre; and new plays by Tony Marchant, David Eldridge, Mark Ravenhill and Phil Willmott. New writing development included a number of works that went to become modern classics including Mark Ravenhill's *Shopping and F***king*, Conor McPherson's *This Lime Tree Bower*, Naomi Wallace's *Slaughter City* and Martin McDonagh's *The Pillowman*.

Since 2000, new British plays have included Laura Wade's London debut with her adaptation of W.H. Davies' *Young Emma*, commissioned for the Finborough Theatre; James Graham's *Albert's Boy* with Victor Spinetti; Sarah Grochala's *S27*; Peter Nichols' *Lingua Franca*, which transferred Off-Broadway; Joy Wilkinson's *Fair*; Nicholas de Jongh's *Plague Over England*; and Jack Thorne's *Fanny and Faggot*, all of which transferred to the West End. Many of the Finborough Theatre's new plays have been published and are on sale from our website.

UK premieres of foreign plays have included Brad Fraser's *Wolfboy*; Lanford Wilson's *Sympathetic Magic*; Larry Kramer's *The Destiny of Me*; Tennessee Williams' *Something Cloudy, Something Clear*; the English premiere of Robert McLellan's Scots language classic, *Jamie the Saxt*; and three West End transfers – Frank McGuinness' *Gates of Gold* with William Gaunt and John Bennett, Joe DiPietro's *F***ing Men* and Craig Higginson's *Dream of the Dog* with Janet Suzman.

Rediscoveries of neglected work have included the first London revivals of Rolf Hochhuth's *Soldiers* and *The Representative*; both parts of Keith Dewhurst's *Lark Rise to Candleford*; *The Women's War*, an evening of original suffragette plays; *Etta Jenks* with Clarke Peters and Daniela Nardini; Noël Coward's first play, *The Rat Trap*; Charles Wood's *Jingo* with Susannah Harker; two sell out productions by J.M. Barrie – *What Every Woman Knows* and *Quality Street*; and Emlyn Williams' *Accolade* with Aden Gillett, Graham Seed and Saskia Wickham.

Music Theatre has included the new (premieres from Grant Olding, Charles Miller, Michael John LaChuisa, Adam Guettel, Andrew Lippa and Adam Gwon – *Ordinary Days* which transferred to the West End) and the old (the UK premiere of Rodgers and Hammerstein's *State Fair* which also transferred to the West End, and the acclaimed *Celebrating British Music Theatre* series, reviving forgotten British musicals).

The Finborough Theatre won *London Theatre Reviews'* Empty Space Peter Brook Award in 2010, the Empty Space Peter Brook Mark Marvin Award in 2004, the Empty Space Peter Brook Award's Dan Crawford Pub Theatre Award in 2005 and 2008 and awards for Best Director and Best Lighting Designer in the 2011 Off West End Awards. It is the only theatre without public funding to be awarded the Pearson Playwriting Award bursary for writers Chris Lee in 2000, Laura Wade in 2005 (who also went on to win the Critics' Circle Theatre Award for Most Promising Playwright, the George Devine Award and an Olivier Award nomination), for James Graham in 2006, for Al Smith in 2007, for Anders Lustgarten in 2009 and Simon Vinnicombe in 2010. Three bursary holders (Laura Wade, James Graham and Anders Lustgarten) have also won the Catherine Johnson Award for Best Play written by a bursary holder. Artistic Director Neil McPherson won the *Fringe Report* Best Artistic Director award in 2009, The Writers' Guild Award for the Encouragement of New Writing in 2010 and Best Artistic Director at the 2011 Off West End Awards.

FINBOROUGH | THEATRE

118 Finborough Road, London SW10 9ED
admin@finboroughtheatre.co.uk
www.finboroughtheatre.co.uk

National
Theatre
Studio

The Leverhulme Bursary for Emerging Directors is a partnership
between the National Theatre Studio and the Finborough Theatre,
supported by The Leverhulme Trust.

The Finborough Theatre is a member of the
Independent Theatre Council, Musical
Theatre Matters UK (MTM:UK) and The Earl's
Court Society www.earlscourtsociety.org.uk

Ecovenue is a European Regional
Development Fund backed three-year
initiative of The Theatres Trust,
aiming to improve the environmental
sustainability of 48 small to medium sized performing arts spaces
across London. www.ecovenue.org.uk

The Finborough Wine Café
Contact Rob Malcolm or Monique Ziervogel on 020 7373 0745 or
finboroughwinecafe@gmail.com

Online
Join us at Facebook, Twitter, MySpace and YouTube.

Mailing
Email admin@finboroughtheatre.co.uk or give your details to our Box Office staff to join our free email list. If you would like to be sent a free season leaflet every three months, just include your postal address and postcode.

Feedback
We welcome your comments, complaints and suggestions.
Write to Finborough Theatre, 118 Finborough Road, London SW10 9ED or email us at admin@finboroughtheatre.co.uk

Friends
The Finborough Theatre is a registered charity. We receive no public funding, and rely solely on the support of our audiences. Please do consider supporting us by becoming a member of our Friends of the Finborough Theatre scheme. There are four categories of Friends, each offering a wide range of benefits.

Richard Tauber Friends – Harry MacAuslan. Brian Smith.
Lionel Monckton Friends – Bridget MacDougall.
William Terriss Friends – Leo and Janet Liebster. Peter Lobl.
Bhagat Sharma. Thurloe and Lyndhurst LLP.

Air Conditioning and Heating Appeal
We are currently fundraising for the cost of the newly installed air conditioning and heating for the auditorium. We are a completely unfunded registered charity. If you would like to make a donation towards the installation of air conditioning, do please speak to the Box Office staff.

Naomi Wallace
And I and Silence

faber and faber

First published in 2011
by Faber and Faber Ltd
74–77 Great Russell Street
London WC1B 3DA

Typeset by Country Setting, Kingsdown, Kent CT14 8ES
Printed in England by CPI Bookmarque, Croydon, Surrey

A CIP record for this book
is available from the British Library

978–0–571–28028–5

2 4 6 8 10 9 7 5 3 1

Characters

Jamie
African American woman, twenty-six

Dee
white woman, twenty-five

Young Jamie
nine years earlier

Young Dee
nine years earlier

Time
1950 and 1959

Place
Somewhere in the USA.

The Past takes place in a cell.

The Present takes place on the outside,
in a city, in a small, mostly bare room.

AND I AND SILENCE

As all the Heavens were a Bell,
And Being, but an Ear,
And I, and Silence, some strange Race
Wrecked, solitary, here —

Emily Dickinson

The Present

In a small room, Jamie and Dee are facing one another, poised, serious. Their room is made up of a minimum of furniture. Jamie is holding a rolled-up newspaper.

Jamie Don't.

Dee I'm gonna do it.

Jamie No.

Dee Can't stop myself.

Jamie I'm not a child any more.

Dee Yeah you are.

Jamie No I'm not.

Dee Been out a whole damn month and waiting on you. Now you're out and already it's getting dark in this room.

Jamie That's not my fault.

Dee I think it is.

Jamie Dee.

Dee Jamie.

Jamie uses the newspaper to threaten Dee.

Jamie I warn you.

Dee (*echoes her*) I warn you.

Jamie Go on. You leave me alone.

Dee When I'm dead.

Suddenly Dee attacks Jamie. At first it seems Dee wants to hurt her, but then we realise she wants to tickle her. Jamie fights hard but she is extremely ticklish. Jamie shrieks and laughs. The newspaper scatters. Jamie says over and over 'Quit!' Finally Dee quits.

You see. It's not dark in here any more. A whole week. You can't go a whole week and not laugh.

Jamie gathers the newspaper together. Both Dee and Jamie are happy, excited.

Jamie There's two in the Highlands. Seen the paper? Big houses. Classy.

Dee Have to be classy.

Jamie They'll need a letter of reference.

Dee Sure. And I'll be your reference. I'll write a letter. I'll write –

Jamie
That Jamie's got a bead for dirt and dust.
She'll polish up your metals, kill the rust.

Jamie straightens up.

Dee
She stands up straight, sure keeps her eyes polite.
She's not stupid but then she's not too bright.

Jamie
No, no, her brain is just the perfect size
And she knows who's the boss, who's always wise.

Dee
She carries her own bucket and a brush,
And she won't say two words if you say –

Jamie Hush.

Dee / Jamie Hush.

Dee 'Cept I still can't write.

Jamie Damn it, Dee.

Dee Ah, forgive a stupid gal, why don't you?

Jamie You had nine years inside to learn. Shame on you. Why didn't you learn?

Dee 'Cause you're the only one I can learn from. You miss me?

Jamie You've been asking me that all week.

Dee And you won't answer me.

Jamie If you'd learned to write you could have wrote me a letter.

Dee Wrote you hundreds. They're all up here.

She taps her forehead.

Why didn't you write me, huh?

Jamie Write what? 'Dear Dee, how's your cell? My cell is just fine. Dark, small, cold, crowded. By the way, I still hate you 'cause you up and got yourself transferred. See you in a few years. Bitch. Love, Jamie.'

Dee Damn. Send that to me again. I love that letter!

Jamie You're still an idiot.

Dee With big teeth.

Jamie Like a horse.

Dee I can do math. I did learn some math.

Jamie Then you can count our dough when it comes in. I'll try for the job in the Highlands. You try for the one on Blankenbaker.

Dee Deal. And you can write my letter of reference.

Jamie But I won't lie.

Dee It's not a lie if it's for a friend.

Jamie considers this.

Jamie
She's half dog, she'll labour to the bone.
Nine years in jail, she needs to turn a stone.
Spent half her time in solitary's hole,
She likes to work at night just like a –

Dee Not a mole. Not a mole!

Jamie shrugs. Dee moves around the room like a boxer.

But I takes orders if you treat me right.
If you cheat me, I'll punch, punch out your light.

Dee boxes the air hard.

I'm dozy, yeah, but hardy as can be.
No finer cleaner you'll come by than me!

Jamie 'Cept for me.

Dee Yeah. 'Cept for you.

Jamie We better wash our dresses. We have to look spiffy for the interview.

Dee gets two buckets of soap and water and places them side by side. Then Dee turns round and Jamie unbuttons her dress. Then Dee unbuttons Jamie's, easily, casually. The women drop their dresses in the buckets. Their movements are almost synchronised. They are wearing knee-length long-johns underneath their dresses to keep warm. They work purposefully, concentrated, as they continue to talk to each other. Then they squeeze out their dresses, and hang them up to dry.

Dee Sharp. Snazzy.

Jamie Clean and new.

Dee And after a few years we'll kick this city to the kerb.

Jamie And get a cabin with a porch.

Dee And rows and rows and rows –

Jamie – of corn.

Dee And a little ole shed that's fat –

Jamie – with chickens. And pigeons on the roof.

Dee And a transistor radio.

Dee belts out a couple of lively lines of her favourite, popular 1950s song. Jamie steps into her bucket.

Jamie My legs, please.

Without hesitation, Dee soaps Jamie's legs, washes them with her hands, easily, practically.

And a husband.

Dee Just like James Stewart. Sturdy and strong.

Jamie Just like James Brown. Ornery and sweet. And you'll marry his brother.

Dee steps into her bucket.

Dee Mine.

Jamie, still in her bucket, washes Dee's legs the same way as they continue to talk. When they are finished, they stand in their buckets looking down at their legs for some moments.

The four of us. Hmm. Livin', workin', cookin' together. Maybe. Maybe.

Jamie I always loved it when you said maybe. 'Cause that always meant yes.

Dee Maybe.

Jamie Say it again.

Dee Nope. Might spoil you.

Jamie is delighted.

Well. Now we're clean.

Jamie Now we're spiffy. Yes.

Dee Yes.

SCENE TWO

The Past

Nine years earlier, in a bare prison cell. Young Jamie is standing alone in her cell, looking out at something we can't see. After some moments, Young Dee enters from another direction. Young Jamie turns slowly and sees her. They say nothing for a long moment, just looking at one another.

Young Jamie I don't know you.

Young Dee We got fifteen minutes –

Young Jamie Get out.

Young Dee – till the bell.

Young Jamie I still don't know you. Git.

Young Dee I've seen you see me.

Young Jamie No.

Young Dee I've seen you. Over and over. (*Beat.*) I'm in cell block four.

Young Jamie White block.

Young Dee Yeah. Don't go eat your lunch.

Young Jamie I'm hungry.

Young Dee Stay.

Young Jamie I like my lunch.

> *Young Jamie tries to get past Young Dee, who blocks her.*

Get outta my way.

Young Dee Can't.

Young Jamie I'll shout.

Young Dee You shout, they'll put us both in the box.

Young Jamie Then move.

Young Dee Trying to get here for weeks.

Young Jamie Don't you touch me.

Young Dee I don't want to touch you. I want –

Young Jamie (*interrupts*) Knew you wanted something.

Young Dee   – to be friends.

Young Jamie Well, I don't.

Young Dee Few months ago, I saw old Mr Crackle the guard knock a bowl of hot chilli right out of your hands.

Young Jamie Chilli's my favourite.

Young Dee Hit the floor, splash.

Young Jamie I picked the bowl up.

Young Dee Yep. But Mr Crackle, he knocked it out of your hands a second time.

Young Jamie And I picked up that bowl again, though there wasn't no chilli in it any more.

Young Dee Me. I would have let it lay. Eight times he knocked that bowl outta your hands. I counted. And you picked it up eight times till Mr Crackle gave in. That's the kind of friend I want.

Young Jamie I don't care what you want and I don't need a friend.

Young Dee I brought you a cigarette.

Young Jamie I don't smoke.

Young Dee Friends bring things. I got peppermint. I'll be seventeen in two months.

Young Jamie I'm already seventeen for five months now, and I don't like peppermint.

Young Dee Hold out your hand.

Young Jamie just shakes her head: 'No.'

You got nine for robbery.

Young Jamie Accessory.

Young Dee I got nine years too.

Young Jamie Don't care.

Young Dee We could do time together.

Young Jamie Already are.

Young Dee Time will go faster.

Young Jamie Not in my mind.

Young Dee We could make something.

Young Jamie just glares at her.

Plans.

Young Jamie I already got plans.

Young Dee For when we get out.

Young Dee notices a small window.

You got a piece of tree. Damn it, I got a brick wall. How'd you get a piece of tree?

Young Jamie Luck likes me.

Young Dee That's a maple.

Young Jamie Oak. Girl can't tell an oak from a maple's no use to me.

Young Dee Not a lot of trees in the city. I can fix a radio.

Young Jamie I can gut a hog.

Young Dee Fix a stove too.

Young Jamie Goat breaks its leg in a hole and it heals bad, I can break it again and mend it. You ever snap a leg 'cross your thigh?

Young Dee Can't say I have.

Young Jamie Can't say you have much then.

They just stare at one another.

Adding to this, you're not smart. You're not smart and you got big teeth.

Young Dee Takes me half the time to chew. (*Beat.*) You ever touch a boy?

Young Jamie Course.

Young Dee How many?

Young Jamie I'm no whore.

Young Dee You a virgin?

Young Jamie Half way.

Young Dee You either are or you aren't.

Young Jamie Don't have to explain to you.

Young Dee One kid that lived next door, and then his brother. But not at the same time. We were at the drive-in, but without the car. You ever been to a drive-in?

Young Jamie just looks away because she hasn't been to a drive-in.

My name's Dee.

Young Jamie Blue eyes make me cold.

Young Dee They say dumb folks with big teeth make good friends.

Too stupid to be late.

Young Jamie
Too stupid to wait.

Young Dee
But they always close the gate.

Young Jamie
Don't know how to hate.

Young Dee
But know how to find
The hole in the mind
Of a friend who lost a brother.

Young Jamie Shut your mouth up.

Young Dee Didn't have no family other than him. He's dead. You're alone. Jamie is all alone. That's what they say.

Young Jamie Hear me, girl. Get the hell out.

Young Dee I'm too dumb to walk away.

They stare each other down.

Young Jamie Friendship's not just peppermints.

A sharp bell sounds. Then it's quiet.

Young Dee I'm sorry about your brother.

Young Jamie Marcel. His name was Marcel.

Young Dee holds out the piece of candy.

Young Dee Look. It a honey drop.

Young Jamie You said it was peppermint. Already you lied.

Young Dee Just testing your forgiveness.

Young Jamie If you can find it, you can test it. Don't lie to me again.

Young Dee Deal.

Young Jamie holds out her hand. After a moment, Young Dee drops the candy in her hand. Young Jamie doesn't look at it, just closes her hand.

Young Jamie We're not friends yet.

SCENE THREE

The Present

Dee in their small room. Jamie enters. Its been raining outside.

Dee You going to congratulate me?

Jamie Why? Oh, you got the job? You got the job!

Dee Yep. I got it. Seven others waiting outside for hours, soaked to the bone. But she chose me.

Jamie is excited.

Jamie Did she ask for a letter?

Dee Before she could ask I gave her three names she could call, memorised the numbers. That impressed her.

Jamie What names? What numbers?

Dee (*shrugs*) Found 'em in a phone book.

Jamie Oh Dee. What if she calls?

Dee I won't give her reason.

Jamie What else?

Dee She asked me what hours. I said –

Jamie 'Any.'

Dee Yep. Asked me about silver. I said – (*imitates the voice*) 'I live to polish, ma'am. Gives me a powerful sense of –

Jamie – achievement.'

Dee Exactly. Asked about my back. If I could lift. She likes it clean under the furniture.

Jamie You said:

Dee 'My back is burly, and while I may not look like an ox, I sure can lift like one.' She raised her eyebrows at that.

Jamie You start tomorrow?

Dee Seven a.m. Your day?

Jamie Washed the curtains. Six rooms. Pile reached the ceiling. She gave me lunch to eat. Leek soup. Delicious. With celery and onions. And a piece of bread.

Dee Hmm.

Jamie takes the bread from her pocket.

Jamie I brought you the bread.

Dee You have it.

Jamie I saved it for you. You didn't eat today.

Dee Not hungry.

Jamie puts the bread back in her pocket.

Jamie It's cold in here.

Dee It's winter out there.

Jamie They got heat in their house.

Dee Mine too. Like July without the bugs.

Jamie They got a television too. While I was cleaning, I snooked a look at *Howdy Doody Time* and caught the end of *Bonanza*.

Dee If she catches you looking . . .

Jamie I know how to look so it looks like looking isn't something I know how to do. (*Beat.*) What's your lady like?

Dee She's tall. Old. Beautiful. She wears big red beads round her neck. Her voice is high and clear. Her son got his leg blowed off in Korea. She says she dreams about his leg following her from room to room. Tap, tap.

Jamie You're lying.

Dee I never lie to you. Damn leg better not follow me around the house.

Jamie That's sad for her.

Dee I told her two legs are not always a necessity. That made her smile. I think she's going to like me.

Jamie The pay?

Dee It'll do. For a start. I bought you something today.

Jamie Don't you buy for me. I told you that. We hardly got enough for rent.

Dee Here.

Dee holds out a long, thin package. After some moments, Jamie relents and takes the package, excited. Jamie takes her time opening it. It's a walking stick. Jamie is suddenly shy.

Jamie That's a beautiful stick.

Dee A real walking stick.

Jamie What kind of tree do you think?

Dee You know I'm no good with trees.

Jamie You didn't ask, when you bought it? Ash. I think its ash.

Dee Maybe.

Jamie Thank you, Dee.

Dee You can walk with it like fancy folks do. Put your chin in the air. Point your toes. Or . . .

Jamie Or?

Dee If we need to do some more practice . . .

Jamie That was years ago.

Dee I might have forgot some things.

Jamie Nah. Just kids when we were locked up together.

Dee There's a lot to remember, if you want to keep up the training, keep up the good work.

Jamie Are you keeping up the good work? Are you presenting yourself as a good worker?

Dee salutes.

Dee The best.

Jamie Show me.

Dee just stares at Jamie. Jamie taps the floor with the stick.

Show me, Miss Dee.

Dee Yes, sir. Would you like a cup of coffee, sir?

Jamie No. I'd like. A piece of cake.

Dee *(as herself)* Give me the bread.

Jamie hands her the piece of bread.

Here's a piece of cake, sir.

Jamie What kind of cake?

Dee Coffee cake. With almonds, sir.

Jamie nibbles the bread.

Jamie This cake is stale. How dare you serve me stale cake!?

Dee But I just baked it.

Jamie Stale! You eat it. You eat it or I'll hit you!

Jamie brandishes the stick. Dee takes the bread and eats it. She's hungry. With satisfaction, Jamie watches her eat.

Wipe your mouth. There are crumbs on your mouth.

Dee wipes her mouth.

Now polish my shoes.

Dee bows.

Dee Of course, sir.

*Dee kneels in front of Jamie. She uses the hem of her
dress to polish Dee's shoes. As Dee polishes, she sings.*

I'm down to the park with my hula hoop
And all the sweet greasers gonna watch me boop.
Get in line, you wanna squeeze my hand.
See me twirl and twist, I'm a marchin' band.

Jamie Straighten my socks.

Dee Yes, sir.

Dee carefully straightens them.

Jamie Lick my knees.

*Dee hesitates. Then she hesitantly gives Jamie's knee a
lick. Jamie shoves her backwards with the stick, hard.*

No! That's the line. That's the line. You say 'No!' You
say 'No!'

Dee But he'll fire me.

Jamie Doesn't matter.

Dee It does.

Jamie We learned this, Dee. Years ago. We can't forget –

Dee – the line. Right. And if he tries to make you lick his
knees then –

Jamie I run and run and run and run. But I don't forget –

Dee – my bucket and brush.

Jamie You never forget your bucket and brush.

*They stare at one another, more content now,
re-energised.*

Dee We both got jobs now.

Jamie Yeah. We can eat. Now we got to find us two
husbands.

Dee Who look like Gary Cooper.

Jamie And can sing like Bo Diddley.

Dee Or Conway Twitty.

Jamie I don't like Twitty.

Dee I don't like Diddley.

They are both silent a moment.

One thing's for sure, they'll have to be brothers so we can –

Jamie / Dee – all live together.

Dee (*drawn out, celebratory*) Yeah.

SCENE FOUR

The Past

Young Jamie in the cell. Alone. Waiting. Waiting. Young Dee finally comes, breathless. Young Jamie doesn't look at her.

Young Dee I couldn't get here.

Young Jamie doesn't respond.

They watch me now.

Young Jamie I can't count on you.

Young Dee Yes you can.

Young Jamie No, I can't. Been months since you first come.

Young Dee Not months. Weeks.

Young Jamie They catch you again they'll move you.

Young Dee Every time I can get away I'll be here. I won't eat – I'll come here.

Young Dee looks up at the window.

Leaves are gone. Did you see 'em go?

Young Jamie Course I did.

Young Dee Oak leaves.

Young Jamie They take longer to fall. Tree won't let 'em go.

Young Dee Selfish. Not like friends.

Young Jamie Might never happen, you and me being friends. (*Beat.*) Besides, you got a friend. White like you. I saw you laughing with her.

Young Dee You didn't see me laugh.

Young Jamie Well.

Young Dee Liar.

Young Jamie I saw you walking with her. In the yard.

Young Dee I don't remember.

Young Jamie I don't forget.

Young Dee I walk when I get the chance, no matter who's at my side.

Young Jamie just shakes her head: 'No.'

Please.

Young Jamie You were in the hole. That's what they say. That why you didn't come?

Young Dee Yeah. But I'm standing here now.

Young Jamie They say you don't sleep. You sit and scream at night.

Young Dee Who says I scream? I'll kick their face.

Young Jamie I never been in the hole. Yet. But I been hit. Me and some girls once we sat up front at dinner time, at your table. Guards hit us on the back till we moved. We got worms in our bowls so fat we name 'em. You and your table get porridge that's clean.

Young Dee Not my fault.

Young Jamie Maybe it is. (*Beat.*) What's it like in the hole?

Young Dee Dark. Like sleep without the hours.

Young Jamie Small?

Young Dee Too crowded if I brought a pet. I don't have a pet.

Young Jamie You shouldn't scream at night.

Young Dee I don't scream, I call. There's a difference.

Young Jamie Who you calling to?

Young Dee You.

Young Jamie Liar.

Young Dee Yep.

Young Jamie Who?

Young Dee None of your business.

They regard one another.

Young Jamie What will we be when we get out?

Young Dee (*no hesitation*) Sailors. They've got the best hats. And live on boats year round.

Young Jamie We could sail to . . . Korea. I like the sound of it.

Young Dee Gonna be a war there.

Young Jamie Too far away.

Young Dee Too far away sounds just the right distance for sailing.

Young Jamie But sailors? We're girls. They'll laugh.

Young Dee I'll hit them.

Young Jamie Sailors get flat feet.

Young Dee I already got flat feet.

Young Jamie I can sew. Make a dress. Can you?

Young Dee A little bit. Shopkeepers? We'll make dresses. Put them in the window.

Young Jamie You got to rent a shop. You got money stashed away?

Young Dee Nope.

Young Jamie Stupid. Neither do I.

Young Dee Bookkeepers?

Young Jamie You can read?

Young Dee Not much. You?

Young Jamie My brother taught me. Fish. We could be fishermen.

Young Dee I don't know how to fish. You'd have to teach me.

Young Jamie I was fishing when I was three. We had a lake.

Young Dee How do you kill a fish?

Young Jamie Marcel did it with a stone, smack to the head.

Young Dee I like that name. Marcel.

Young Jamie Marcel could whistle any tune on the radio. He could whistle violins, tubas, banjos. He was an orchestra. (*Beat.*) That's what my mother said. (*Beat.*) He had a piece of wood in his pocket, made it look like a gun. We went into that grocery store together. Man in the store had a real gun. Shot Marcel in the neck.

Young Dee And you got nine years.

Young Jamie What you in for?

Young Dee You know why.

Young Jamie Rumours.

Young Dee Believe them. (*Beat.*) So what we gonna be?

Young Jamie My momma was a parlourmaid.

Young Dee A servant?

Young Jamie She called herself a parlourmaid. Took a bus to the city every morning. Me and Marcel, we worked the field while she was gone.

Young Dee What was her name?

Young Jamie Betty. Raised me and Marcel up on her own.

Young Dee She dead?

Young Jamie Drowned.

Young Dee In the lake?

Young Jamie Cleaning floors.

Young Dee laughs briefly. Then realises Young Jamie is not playing.

Young Dee You can't drown cleaning floors.

Young Jamie One time I found her on the kitchen floor. One time on the porch. She had blackouts. Ever since she was a girl. She must of had one and fell with her face in the bucket. That's how they found her. Me and Marcel went to get her body where she worked. I asked for her pay. Gave us half a week, said she hadn't worked past Wednesday.

Young Dee Do you want a honey drop?

Young Dee gives her one and she takes it, putting it in her pocket.

We could be servants. We could be like Betty.

Young Jamie She made enough to feed us.

Young Dee All we need is enough.

Young Jamie Sometimes she took me with her. I watched her work.

Young Dee Then you know how it goes.

Young Jamie It's a speciality. Might take a long time to teach it.

Young Dee Good.

Young Jamie You don't need much.

Young Dee A bucket?

Young Jamie Two buckets. With strong handles. One for each of us.

Young Dee Rags?

Young Jamie And soap.

Young Dee Water.

Young Jamie Lots of water. And a clean dress. You got to look professional. If you're dirty they think you can't clean. Got to be spiffy.

Young Dee Spiffy.

Young Jamie Ironed.

Young Dee Crisp. Fresh.

Young Jamie Sparkling!

Young Dee Bingo. That's settled then. We'll be servants. Work the finest houses. Get paid in cash!

Young Jamie Get leftovers!

Young Dee Get hand-me-downs!

Young Jamie Get anything they throw away!

The young women rejoice, then Young Jamie sings.

Ma'am . . .
If you don't want that thing no more,
I'll take it home, 'cause I so poor.
And you so kind, your heart so big.
If you're sweet to me, I'll dance a jig!

Young Jamie does a jig as she chants. Young Dee claps in time.

I'll take those socks, I can mend that hole,
On that broke chair, I'll rest my bones.
A piece of glass, ma'am, I can use that too.
A dress that's stained to me is new.

Now Young Jamie claps in time and Young Dee jigs.

Young Dee (*sings*)
I'll have that broken birthday toy.
That rug with burns, it'll bring me joy.
Oh let me kiss your generous hand,
What's garbage to you, to me is grand!

Now the two young women dance together. The harsh sound of the bell interrupts their pleasure. They stop dancing. It's quiet again.

Young Jamie But we'll have to practise.

Young Dee Yeah. Practise.

SCENE FIVE

The Present

Dee in their small room. Standing still, waiting. Jamie enters, tired.

Dee Russell came by again.

Jamie perks up, excited.

Jamie He did?

Dee He did.

Jamie Tell me.

Dee What's to tell?

Jamie Come on, Dee!

Dee Nothing to tell.

Jamie What'd he say?

Dee Didn't say much.

Jamie He leave a message?

Dee No message.

Jamie (*crestfallen*) No message . . . You're lying!

Dee I don't lie.

Jamie Yes, you do.

Dee He's short. Russell is short.

Jamie Dee.

Dee (*imitates Russell*) 'Where's that Jamie girl?'

Jamie (*laughs, delighted*) I knew it. I knew it! Did you tell him what time I'd be home?

Dee I told him you didn't live here any more.

Jamie You didn't.

Dee Yep.

Jamie You didn't.

Dee No. I said, 'Jamie'll be back after eight.' (*Beat.*) And then I added, 'She thinks you're short.'

Jamie No. What did he –

Dee He said, 'Short's got nothing to do with style.'

Jamie Good. Good. I like his style. Shut you up, didn't he? He's a shopkeeper.

Dee He's a rascal. Just wants to bed you.

Jamie Uh-uh. You're wrong.

Dee You take your pants off for him and see if he comes back.

Jamie First time me and Russell went out he gave me a present. Not a lot of men do that for you. Gave me a spoon and a fork.

Dee Shit.

Jamie Nah, silver. Pretty. Little buds on the top.

Dee Utensils. He gives you utensils. Stacking your drawer so you can feed him when he moves in.

Jamie He doesn't want to move in. He's got his own place.

Dee So he says. You kiss him yet?

Jamie Not your business.

Dee He's got short teeth.

Jamie Well, he's a short man.

Dee No. I mean little bitty teeth, mouth of a –

Jamie (*interrupts*) Don't say it!

Dee – reptile.

Jamie just studies Dee.

I'm just looking out for you. If I could earn money doing
that –

Jamie (*interrupts*) I've got potatoes. Onions. We can
make soup.

Dee What happened at work?

Jamie Same thing.

Dee You talk nice? You smile?

Jamie Sure, honey. I smile. I talk nice.

Dee Yeah.

Jamie He said: 'Could you clean the basement floor?'
I said:

Dee 'Clean it so nice your chile can eat off it, sir.'

Jamie Show me.

Dee He said –

Jamie 'Show me' and followed me into the basement. It
was a pretty floor from door to door.

Dee And then.

Jamie He came up behind me –

Dee Touched –

Jamie – me. Yes.

Dee I'll kill him.

Jamie That's what you always say.

Dee You're my best friend.

Jamie You'll ever have. That's the truth. But he didn't get nothing 'cause I ran. Didn't forget my bucket and brush. But I'm outta work now.

Dee I'll try for another job tomorrow. There's one advertised full time. Pearl Avenue. You stay home a while. Get some rest.

Jamie After these potatoes we got nothing.

Dee I'll hold on to this job.

Jamie You do that.

Dee I'll be more polite this time. I'll say –

Jamie Yes, sir.

Dee Yes, ma'am.

Jamie / Dee At your service.

Jamie I took off my pants for Russell.

They are both silent some moments.

One afternoon last week when you were out. So you're wrong, 'cause he had me and he came back.

Dee says nothing.

I asked him if he had a brother but he hasn't got a brother. He's got a cousin though. Name's Charles.

Dee Huh. And what's Charles look like?

Jamie Well, I asked Russell and he said, 'Charles has a good neck.'

Dee A good neck? What about the rest of him?

Jamie Russell didn't tell me about the rest of him.

Dee So Charlie's got a good neck. What the hell is a good neck, Jamie?

Jamie I don't know.

Dee Jesus, he must be ugly.

Jamie We could double-date.

Dee just looks at her.

We could. (*Beat.*) You bothered 'cause he's black?

Dee He care if I'm white?

Jamie Not the same thing.

Dee The four of us can't go out on the town. Too dangerous.

Jamie Not if they come over here. We can serve drinks. Candied peanuts. Or-derves. (*Beat.*) Please.

Dee considers for some moments.

Please.

Dee Sure. Okay. Tell Russell I'll go out with his cousin's neck if he leaves the rest behind.

Jamie (*laughing*) We could have some fun.

Dee Maybe.

Jamie Please, Dee.

Dee Maybe. Yeah. We could have some fun.

Jamie Yes! Yes! I'll tell Russell to set it up. Thank you, Dee. Thank you. This is what we planned. This is what we always planned and it's coming our way.

The women just look at one another.

Dee Every time you walk in that door.

Jamie Yeah. Me too.

The Past

Young Dee and Young Jamie in the cell.

Young Dee Seems pretty simple to me. Bucket. Rag. Simple.

Young Jamie Bucket and rag got nothing to do with it. These are not essentials. Essentials is your style.

Young Dee Teach me.

Young Jamie Heard they gonna move you.

Young Dee Don't listen to 'em.

Young Jamie You in the hole three times. One more time and they move you to maximum.

Young Dee Nobody's gonna move me.

Young Jamie Once in the hole for coming here. One time for screaming. You can't get in trouble again. We got years left.

Young Dee Eight.

Young Jamie And a half. You got to stop it, Dee. You got to act right. What you do this time?

Young Dee Nothing. Christ.

Young Jamie Dee.

Young Dee At breakfast there's this guard, Monkfish, we call him, on account of his smell. Well, Monkfish he comes to the table and he drinks my juice. Why's he got

35

to drink *my* juice every morning? Why not spread it around? They do that at your table?

Young Jamie Sometimes. But juice don't matter.

Young Dee Mine does.

Young Jamie Now eggs matter. Eggs got substance. I get slapped for hiding my eggs when the guard wants them. But I don't ever give them up.

Young Dee Well, I like juice. I wake at daybreak and I think 'juice'. So one mornin' I pour my juice into the girl's next to me, then I put my cup under the table and I piss in it.

Young Jamie No!

Young Dee Yes. Then I put the cup right there on my tray, waiting for Monkfish. He leans over me like he always does, buttons on his uniform brushin' my neck, my face. Picks up the cup and drinks deep.

Young Jamie (*clapping her hands*) Oh no! Oh no, Dee!

Young Dee Yep.

Young Jamie Did he drink it?

Young Dee All the way down. Then his face turned pucker and his eyes go wide.

Young Jamie All the way down!

Young Dee Best moment of my life.

Young Jamie He hit you.

Young Dee Didn't stop till I passed out. But I was floating I was so damn glad.

Young Jamie Weeks in the hole.

Young Dee Months would have been worth it.

Young Jamie Monkfish take your juice again when you got out?

Young Dee Won't come near my table.

Young Jamie laughs.

Only minutes now. Let's work.

Young Jamie Sure then. Start with dusting. You'll need a –

Young Dee – rag.

Young Jamie Yes. A rag. But you got to use it right. Because whoever's gonna hire you, they gonna watch you. They watch to see if you love your work. Now you hold your cloth – (*beat*) like a bird.

Young Dee Never held a bird.

Young Jamie Be quiet. I'm teaching you. You hold it. Like a bird.

Young Jamie demonstrates.

Young Dee Betty teach you this?

Young Jamie Yes, she did, and she knew.

Young Dee What kind of bird you holdin'?

Young Jamie What kind?

Young Dee Yeah. There's different kinds of birds. Big. Scrawny. Yellow. Black.

Young Jamie It don't matter.

Young Dee Everything matters.

Young Jamie All right. Then it's a . . . robin.

Young Dee Too puny. How about a crow?

Young Jamie Crows are mean.

Young Dee Maybe that's what you need when you swipe. Swipe.

Young Jamie Fine. You hold it like a – crow. You hold it and let it flitter its wings across the dust.

Young Dee Flitter.

Young Jamie Flitter.

Young Dee You're makin' this up.

Young Jamie How dare you?

Young Dee Sorry. Go on.

Young Jamie You want to be a servant, you got to have something no other servant's got. Grace. Good cheer. Style. And flitter.

Young Dee Give me that rag.

Young Jamie Give me that *crow*.

Young Dee Yeah. So I can wring its neck.

Young Jamie This crow is your friend. Its wing will flick the dust away.

Young Dee You said flitter. Now you're saying flick.

Young Jamie Its wing will flick. And flitter the dust from the furniture. And if they're watching you, hating you – and they hate you 'cause they mad they got to pay you – they'll think: hmm. This one's different. She enjoys her work. She's got –

Young Jamie / Young Dee – style.

Young Jamie holds the rag out to Young Dee. Young Dee takes the cloth gingerly, awkwardly, as though it were a wing.

Young Jamie Do the bookshelves.

Young Dee looks around, 'sees' some imaginary bookshelves and dusts them, leaning over.

Don't hunch when you dust. If you got to do the bookshelves low down, curtsy as you dust. Like this.

Young Jamie shows Young Dee how to do it.

Young Dee Huh.

Young Dee tries, not very well.

Young Jamie That's a bend, not a curtsy. Don't ever bend. Over.

Young Dee Why?

Young Jamie A good servant is always graceful.

Young Jamie shows her grace, flitting about the cell, dusting with 'style'. Young Dee watches her, fascinated.

Young Dee So if I do this I not only get the job but I keep it.

Young Jamie quits dusting.

Young Jamie Exactly.

Young Dee I never liked birds.

Young Jamie You like trees.

Young Dee Just maples.

Young Jamie They go together, birds and trees. You can't have one without the other. And you can't learn to dust right thinking about rags. You can only dust right thinking about flitter. Flitter lives in the mind. Flitter and dust, they go together. You put rags in your mind, you got nothing.

The Present

Dee is lying on her back on the bed, staring. Jamie has just come home from work.

Jamie Did Russell come by?

Dee Each time you ask me that and each time I say no.

Jamie Charlie come by?

Dee Now why would Charlie come by?

Jamie Well. You kissed him when we doubled.

Dee I did not. He kissed me and I let him.

Jamie You liked it.

Dee Yeah, I did, but I didn't think much of his neck. I don't know why Russell brags about it.

Jamie Russell's married.

Dee Oh.

Jamie He told me. Afterwards.

Dee The bastard. I'll hit him.

Jamie We had some nice times.

Dee You in love with him?

Jamie Don't be silly. He's a stupid man. But I like him 'cause he knows it.

Dee I'm stupid.

Jamie No, you're not.

Dee In prison, you always said I was stupid.

Jamie I was encouraging you.

Dee So I'm smart?

Jamie Yep. And I like you 'cause you don't know it. (*Beat.*) You sick again, Dee?

Dee No. Just resting.

Jamie Lately you're always resting.

Dee Nah. I just like looking at the ceiling and waiting on you to come home.

Jamie Did you sleep?

Dee Yeah. (*Beat.*) I dreamed I fucked my mother.

Silence some moments.

Jamie Oh. How many times?

Dee Just once.

Jamie The dream or –

Dee Both. Do you find me disgusting?

Jamie just looks at her for some moments. Dee waits.

Jamie I find you sleeping. Every time I get home.

Dee She was alive in the dream, my mother. I went down on her.

Jamie (*firmly but quietly*) That's enough.

Dee In the dream I was sixteen again. I lay so close to her. It had nothin' to do with fuckin'. My mother, she was – radiant. Her hands weren't broken. More than I did then, I miss her now.

Jamie Be quiet.

Dee I can't sleep.

Jamie You just told me you were napping.

Dee In the day. Like today. But at night I can't sleep.

Jamie You should take the bed. I can sleep on the floor.

Dee Wouldn't matter.

Jamie When I wake in the dark, I can tell you're awake by how you breathe.

Dee I'm always awake in the dark.

Jamie You'll keep the next job.

Dee But it's not a waking in the dark. The waking *is* the dark.

Jamie Whole neighbourhood's out of work. It's not just you. Don't feel sorry for yourself.

Jamie gets Dee a cup of water.

Dee I won't, if you'll do it for me.

Jamie That'd be a disrespect.

Dee I'd like a little if it comes from you.

Jamie Drink the water.

Dee drinks.

We'll lose this place if it keeps on this way.

Dee We were happy when we were inside. Sometimes.

Jamie When we were together. They kept us apart.

Dee We found a way to meet. Here, we can't go out together. We can't sit together. We can't walk together any more.

Jamie We can walk together.

Dee Then why don't we?

Jamie You know why.

Dee Sure. 'Cause folks on the street see us together, everyone thinks you're my maid. Me, have a maid? How could I ever afford a maid?

Jamie That's not the point.

Dee We walk on down Oak Street, go into BB-Jigs hardware for a light bulb. The guy who looks like Mr Potato Head's Uncle with a pipe asks and asks how we know each other so we say that really you're not my servant. But he doesn't believe us, so we tell Mr Potato Head's Uncle the truth: that we're both servants. That we're friends. What do we get then?

Jamie Be quiet.

Dee What do we get? An orange crush bottle flying through the air. Then another 'cross my back. Guts from the butcher in your hair. Doors slamming behind us –

Jamie (*interrupts*) Quit your whinin'. Guts in my hair is nothing. Bottle 'cross my back is nothing. I walk the street alone to work I never know what's flying through the air. Pisspot from the second floor. Dog shit. People cursin' me, white people, your people, stick out a leg and trip me.

Dee They're not my people.

Jamie Oh yeah they are. When you want them to be.

Dee Not that easy for me either.

Jamie But when you walk to work you okay, Dee. You okay. It's only when you walk with me you in trouble.

Dee I wish I could kill people and get away with it.

Jamie just shakes her head in exasperation.

When we were inside at least our bellies were full.

Jamie Not often enough.

Dee We got to see each other and we weren't hungry. Could take our minds off eatin'. Use our minds for other things. Now, we got nothing. We got to start. Taking things.

Jamie Taking things? You mean stealin'? (*Beat.*) If they send me back, I'll be alone.

Dee I'll go with you.

Jamie Not likely we'd go to the same place again. That was luck the first time.

Dee gets up.

Dee I shit on luck. You go back in, I go back in.

Jamie is silent.

You sad about Russell?

Jamie turns away.

Don't be sad about Russell. And those itty-bitty teeth.

Jamie doesn't answer.

Only man worth a kiss is a man who's got teeth like a horse.

Jamie I'll make us something to eat.

Dee Russell found a piece of – treasure when he found you. Gonna be a poor man now for the rest of his life. I almost feel sorry for him.

Jamie just looks at Dee for a moment, grateful for the compliment.

Jamie It's soup again.

Dee Soup for weeks now. I hate soup.

Jamie Well, I don't think it likes you either, Dee, 'cause you always disrespect it. But after the rent it's all we can afford.

Dee Our strategy's gone stale.

Jamie No. You just got to find another job. Think about that field we're gonna plant.

Dee That just makes me hungrier.

Jamie And rows and rows of okra. And beets –

Dee – as big as my fist. Melons as sweet as a baby's ass.

Jamie And quail. They make fancy eggs, quail. (*Beat.*) You're right about Russell's teeth. Those itty-bitty teeth too small to go clink-clink on mine.

Jamie laughs, but stops abruptly.

Dee You eat the soup.

Jamie Please, Dee.

Dee (*warning*) Leave me alone.

SCENE EIGHT

The Past

The cell. Young Jamie and Young Dee are practising.

Young Dee I said: I'm thirsty.

After a moment's hesitation, Young Jamie takes off her shoe, using it as a cup.

Young Jamie Ma'am. I brought you your cup of hot milk.

Young Dee Thank you, dear. Now help me drink it.

45

Young Jamie brings the 'cup' to Young Dee, holding it out with two hands.

To my lips.

Young Jamie carefully brings the 'cup' to Young Dee's lips. Young Dee 'drinks'.

Again.

Young Jamie does so again. Young Dee drinks.

Enough.

Young Jamie moves away.

Now don't forget.

Young Jamie Don't forget what?

Young Dee Have you forgot?

Young Jamie Yes. I think I have.

Young Dee (*as herself*) Should I get the stick?

Young Jamie Not yet.

Young Dee You tell me when.

Young Jamie (*as a servant again*) What did I forget, ma'am?

Young Dee Something real important.

Young Jamie But I don't know what I forgot. (*Whispers, as herself.*) Now get the stick.

Young Dee gets the 'stick', which is a thin, strong piece of wood, three feet long.

Young Dee I don't want a maid that can't remember.

Young Jamie But I can. If you help me.

Young Dee You are a real. Dis-ap-pointment.

Young Dee suddenly switches Young Jamie on the legs with the stick, but not hard.

Young Jamie I'm sorry, ma'am.

Young Dee What was I thinking to hire you . . .

Young Dee hits Young Jamie again, just a little bit harder.

Young Jamie But how can I learn if you're so strict, ma'am?

Young Dee It's strict that will tighten your mind.

Hits her again.

Young Jamie (*as herself*) Dee, help me.

Young Dee Too late, you're fired.
Walk to the door.
Walk to the door, whore.

Young Jamie walks a few steps away.

Young Jamie But there is no door.

Young Dee Don't –

Young Jamie It's true.

Young Dee – ever say that. Don't ever. Look. I'll give you a hint.
After he drinks, after she drinks, you do what?

Young Jamie still doesn't know.

South end of the face is . . .?

Young Jamie (*gets it*) Your mouth! I forgot to wipe her mouth. After she drank.

Young Jamie slowly moves to Young Dee and with her fingers wipes Young Dee's lips, carefully, but professionally. Then Young Jamie steps away.

It's raining outside.

Young Dee Yep. And cold.

Young Jamie January.

Young Dee The water is frozen over. Kids are putting on their skates. Will the ice hold?

They have switched roles again.

Young Jamie Me, I'm looking at the door again. I'm thinking I've made a mistake in hiring this weak, skinny white girl.

Young Dee No. You haven't made a mistake. I'm hardy. I got a grip.

Young Jamie But you don't ever sing!

Young Dee Not while I work.

Young Jamie (*as herself*) Listen. If he asks you to sing, you got to sing. That's why we learn the songs. In case they ask us to sing while we dust. Sing while we polish. They like to hear us happy when we work. You only need one song. You can vary it.

Young Dee Did Betty have a song when she worked?

Young Jamie Yep. She made it up for me.

Young Dee Sing it.

Young Jamie It was mine, from her, especially.

Young Dee Don't matter. We can learn it and sing it.

Young Jamie is unsure.

And then it won't be forgot.

Young Jamie (*sings, teaching Young Dee*)
I'm down to the park with my hula hoop
And all the sweet greasers gonna watch me boop.
Get in line, you wanna squeeze my hand.
See me twirl and twist, I'm a marchin' band.

Young Dee Huh. How about 'Frog went a-Courtin'?

Young Jamie That's not sophisticated.

Young Dee Neither is my memory. (*Beat.*) I could learn the last lines and sing it over and over. (*Sings, unsure.*)

I'm down to the park with my hula hoop . . .

Young Jamie
And all the sweet greasers gonna watch me boop.

Young Jamie helps Young Dee with the lines.

Young Dee / Young Jamie
Get in line, you wanna squeeze my hand.

Young Jamie Go on.

Young Dee (*sings*)
See me twirl and twist, I'm a marchin' band.

Young Jamie While you dust.

Young Dee takes up position to dust.

Young Dee
I'm down to the park with my hula hoop
And all the greasers gonna watch me boop.

Young Dee gets into the rhythm of the dusting and singing, repeating her phrase, indulging in it.

Young Jamie Stop.

Young Dee keeps singing and dusting.

I said stop!

Young Dee stops, just looks at Young Jamie.

You said 'all the greasers'.

Young Dee Yeah.

Young Jamie It's 'all the *sweet* greasers'.

Young Dee Oh.

Young Jamie now slips the stick from Young Dee's hand.

Young Jamie You dropped a word.

Young Dee I can pick it back up.

Young Jamie Once you drop a word that's supposed to have a place, it's gone.

Young Dee Where's it gone to?

Young Jamie A word hole.

Young Dee That's crazy.

Young Jamie And you can spit and spit but it won't come back out again. You get one chance with a word. You misuse that chance, you don't get another. (*Beat.*) And when that happens, they kick you to the kerb.

Young Dee I'm sorry.

Young Jamie It's too late. You messed up.

Young Dee Yes. I did.

Young Jamie hits Young Dee sharply on the legs with the stick. The hitting with the stick is more intense now.

Young Jamie You were clumsy.

Young Jamie hits her again.

Young Dee I was clumsy. I dropped –

Young Jamie – a word.

Young Dee Down the hole it went. Can't ever get it out again. (*Beat.*) But I didn't just drop the word. I dropped the knife. After I –

Young Dee won't continue.

Young Jamie Say it, Dee. Say it now.

Young Dee I can't.

Young Jamie strikes her three times while speaking.

Young Jamie Yes, you can. Say it. Say it.

Young Dee does not flinch. She is silent some moments, then calmly speaks.

Young Dee In the city. Outside our apartment. There were stairs. When I left for school, when I returned, I'd count them.

Young Dee stalls.

Young Jamie (*encouraging her*) You'd count them.

Young Dee Seventeen steps up, seventeen steps down. My mother would hide her wages. Keep something back for her and me. He'd hit her every time she did it and she did it every time.

Young Dee stalls again.

Young Jamie Seventeen steps up . . .

Young Dee And seventeen steps down. One night he threw her down the stairs and she tried to stop herself falling and both her hands broke at the wrist. Snap. Snap. When she stood up, she held her arms out to me. I ran to her but her hands were just – Hanging off her wrists. She couldn't hold me. I stuck a bread knife in his side.

After a moment.

Young Jamie You loved your father.

Young Dee No. But I loved him.

Silence some moments.

Young Jamie Robin. That was your mother's name.

Young Dee How do you know?

Young Jamie It's the name you call in your sleep. That's what they say.

Young Dee Robin.

Young Jamie Robin and Dee.

The bell sounds sharply.

Young Dee Next time I come, can we polish the silver?

Young Jamie Sure.

Young Dee Is it beautiful, the silver?

Young Jamie Vases and mirrors and candelabras.

Young Dee Can-del-a . . . bras.

Young Jamie You'll have to know how to say it. 'Ma'am, I've finished polishing the candelabras.'

Young Dee I did it with a flitter, ma'am.

Young Jamie No, no. Silver you polish with a swick, swick.

Young Dee Swick.

Young Jamie It's all in the elbow.

Young Dee Jamie. I've never been so –

Young Jamie Me either.

Young Dee Even when I was out there.

Young Jamie Me either.

Young Dee In here it's like hell but all I feel now is –

Young Jamie – happy.

The Present

Jamie and Dee in their small room. Jamie has her back to Dee.

Dee Jamie.

No answer.

Jamie.

Jamie I don't know you.

Dee Hey.

Jamie Get away from me.

Dee I'm your friend.

Jamie Then wash your hands. Wash 'em!

Dee I already did.

Jamie Do it again.

Dee Jamie.

Jamie Don't say my name.

Dee washes her hands again, vigorously.

I keep seeing it. I keep seeing it in my head.

Dee Well, don't. See me.

Jamie There it is. In my head again.

Dee dries her hands.

Dee Look at me. Look at me. See *me*.

Jamie You crossed the line.

Dee I'm your best friend.

Jamie crosses quickly to Dee and slaps her hard in the face. Dee takes it.

I bought you something.

Jamie Don't you dare.

Dee I did. Candy Corn.

Jamie I don't want it.

Dee You'll forget. I'll forget.

Jamie We're supposed to remember.

Dee Not all things.

Jamie What were you thinking? What the hell were you thinking?

Dee No one's hiring. City's howling it's that cold. Both of us hungry. You been out of work weeks now. Then I got lucky. Working for a gentleman in Hunting Creek, a handsome man. Pretty wife too. She didn't ask me to lift the heavy furniture. The wages were enough to pay the back rent. Of you. I was thinking of you.

Jamie You say it was for me and I'll –

Dee – kill you. Don't mind if it's you.

Jamie moves away.

Jamie We got soup for dinner.

Dee No, we don't. Stop lying. We haven't had soup for three days. There's no money. We've got a couple more weeks here then they'll kick us out.

Jamie Then what are we going to do?

Dee Nothing. Let's do nothing. Both of us. (*Beat.*) Ever again.

Jamie What do you mean?

Dee I can't go out there any more. Not without you. I can't do it. You can't either. We should. Quit. Just quit.

Jamie takes this in some moments, in silence.

Jamie I want to live.

Dee Like this? Like this? You want to fuckin' live like this?

Jamie (*angry*) You should be ashamed.

Dee Well, I've been thinking about it.

Jamie For how long?

Dee ignores her.

For how long have you been thinking about it?

Dee There's no place for us.

Jamie Yes there is.

Dee The streets don't want us.

Jamie That'll change.

Dee Bullshit.

Jamie So is what you're thinkin'.

Dee But it's quiet there. I know it's got to be quiet there. Don't you want that? I know there's a part of you wants that quiet.

Jamie It's wrong to talk like this.

Dee But you and me we always wanted to travel. It'll be – a kind of travel.

Jamie Only we can't come back.

Dee We won't want to come back, Jamie. From a place where . . . There's no cold 'cause winter forgot what cold was. And no wind 'cause it's laid down to sleep. Where

55

there's no being hungry and the dark is just something easy you can shake from your hair. That world is ours.

Jamie just listens to Dee, then to the silence around them.

Jamie Right here, there's still trees. And to look at them.

Dee We can't eat trees.

Jamie There's the weather. To make our skin wet.

Dee That's romance.

Jamie No. That's rain. (*Beat.*) You think you're the only one? You think I don't know that everything we planned is behind us? You're right. I can't get quiet in my head. Nothin' in my skull but loose change, rattlin', rattlin', and it don't stop. But I'm not gonna stop. Givin' up, it's gutless.

Dee Yeah, but I'm gonna stop, Jamie. I'm gonna stop. Are you with me?

Jamie Go to hell. I don't give up, remember? I never have.

Dee Close your eyes. Close your eyes!

Jamie closes her eyes. Dee circles her, talking.

Feel that? Quiet. All over you. And somewhere there's something falling easy on you. Sand. Water. But soundless. Yeah. It'll be just like that. Its not a givin' up. Its a givin' in, to a world where we almost are. Almost. Are.

Jamie stays with her eyes closed.

I love you.

Jamie opens her eyes.

Jamie How dare you.

Dee That's all I need. Just knowing that.

Jamie Don't ever say that to me again.

Dee I love you.

Jamie begins to laugh but there is fear in her laugh. Then she stops.

Do you love me?

Jamie We got to eat. That's all this is. You're just light headed from not eatin'.

Dee Answer me.

Jamie We need to eat. We have a right to eat.

Dee I can't eat. Not ever again.

Jamie Why?

Dee Because of my mouth. It's gone.

Jamie You're crazy. I can see your mouth.

Dee No, you can't.

Jamie Your mouth is not gone.

Dee You are a liar.

Jamie I never lied.

Dee Yes, you did. You let them touch you.

Jamie Only on top of my dress. Not ever under it.

Dee They squeezed you.

Jamie Under the cloth I was safe.

Dee They rubbed you.

Jamie They didn't ever touch my skin. And with the money I got, we ate for weeks.

Dee When I'm down on my hands and knees all I can think of. When I'm a servant, all I can think of.

Jamie Is what?

Dee All I can think of is Jamie. On her knees on the floor, back curved, hands wet. I won't do it any more. We got to. Go away.

Jamie This. Is. Away. Right here.

Dee shakes her head.

I'm going to ask our neighbour for food.

Dee Again? You got no pride.

Jamie More than you'll ever know.

Dee I doesn't matter: I can't eat.

Jamie Yes, you can.

Dee When he came in my mouth, he boxed my ears. Didn't mean to, he said, it just felt so damn good. I got off my knees. My head was ringing. I left my bucket and brush.

Jamie You left your bucket and brush? How could you? How could you!?

Dee just shakes her head. Jamie gets the stick.

You will tell me how.

Dee keeps her mouth shut. Jamie hits Dee. Dee takes the blow. Jamie hits her again, harder.

Show me how, Miss Dee. You damn well show me.

Dee slowly sinks to her knees.

Dee No, sir.

Jamie hits her again with the stick.

Jamie I only take yes in this house.

Dee No, sir. Please.

Jamie This is the last time I'm asking you.

Dee I need this job, sir.

Jamie Then do as I say.

Dee I got a friend at home. She's laid off again. We got rent to pay.

Jamie Do as I say!

Dee But there's a line. Years and years we learned it. Me and Jamie. Please, sir. Hear me.

Jamie Open my damn belt!

Jamie strikes her again, harder. After a moment, Dee very slowly begins to open the belt on Jamie's dress. Now Jamie speaks as herself.

This is what you did, Dee?

Dee Yes.

Jamie After what we promised each other? How to stop it? How to get up and walk away? This is what you did?

Dee Yes.

Jamie You're not my friend.

Dee (*quietly*) Always.

Jamie And then what? Then what did you do?

Dee I opened my mouth.

Jamie (*as herself*) Oh my God.

Dee And then he stuck it in.

Jamie (*as the 'gentleman'*) Do it. Do it.

Suddenly Dee takes Jamie's hand and forces Jamie's fingers into her mouth. Dee gags and gags but doesn't resist.

You take it. That's right. You take it, Miss Dee. Don't you gag. Don't you gag. Suck me. Suck me, you whore!

Dee now finds her breath and begins to suck Jamie's fingers/hand. Jamie closes her eyes. We can hear Dee sucking Jamie's fingers. Jamie now speaks as herself.

I feel it. It's not gone.

Jamie is crying, but almost silently.

Dee. Your mouth. It's not gone.

Dee suddenly removes Jamie's fingers and wrenches open Jamie's dress. Dee buries her face in Jamie, between her legs. Jamie holds her tight, tighter.

SCENE TEN

The Past

Young Dee and Young Jamie in the cell. Young Jamie quietly watches Young Dee.

Young Jamie Why didn't you tell me?

Young Dee Tell you what?

Young Jamie Don't pretend.

Young Dee I didn't tell you because I'm not going.

Young Jamie Fourth time in the hole, they ship you up state now.

Young Dee No one is shipping me anywhere.

Young Jamie Nothing you can do to stop it.

Young Dee Then I'll be good, so they'll send me back here quick.

Young Jamie You'll serve out your time there. We won't ever see each other again. Every day that passes, every week, I'll hate you for ruining our plans.

Young Dee In seven years we'll both be out.

Young Jamie You'll forget in seven years.

Young Dee No. I won't. I'll practise every day. Everything we learned. And when we get out, we'll meet up and walk into the city arm in arm in the hot summertime, down Oak Street and past the park, buy some doughnuts at Patsy's Pies and two sodas so cold they'll freeze our gums. Maybe I'll buy me some blue suede shoes, and a bottle of perfume like a daffodil, for you. That's a fact.

Young Jamie You'll find other friends.

Young Dee You'll find other friends.

Young Jamie I hope so.

Young Dee But none of them will be me: Dee.

Young Jamie Dee and Jamie.

Young Dee You and me. My uncle's got rooms to rent, real cheap. Only one window but there's a lock on the door. No water but we can haul it in from the hydrant.

Young Jamie But seven years?

Young Dee Just seven years. It'll go by that fast. We'll be older.

Young Jamie Taller. Sophisticated.

Young Dee We'll be. Candelabras. (*Beat.*) I swear. I swear, Jamie. Do you?

After some moments Jamie answers.

Young Jamie Yes. I do. I swear.

Young Dee grabs Young Jamie and twirls her around. They laugh and spin.

Young Dee (*sings*)
And on, on down to the picture shows,
On Sunday if it really snows,
I'll buy you a bag of candy,
Pink and green and red and tangy.

Young Jamie / Young Dee (*sing*)
Arm in arm
We'll stay real warm,
'Cause its cold out there
Even when the weather's fair.

The women are dizzy. They quit and recover. Stillness floats between them.

Young Dee Jamie. Jamie. Jamie.

Young Jamie Keep saying it.

Young Dee keeps saying her name.

SCENE ELEVEN *and* SCENE TWELVE

The Present

Jamie and Dee in the room. They have not left it in days. Jamie sits on the bed. Dee is standing some distance away from her.

Jamie I saw my brother Marcel again. He still had the hole in his neck from the bullet, but it wasn't bleeding. I put my hand to his neck and there was cold air blowing out the hole. But the cold was a kind of tune. Pipes and horns. Then I woke.

Dee You want some water?

Jamie No.

Dee I'll get a cup.

Jamie Water ran out two days ago. Kiss my fingers, Dee.

Dee goes to Jamie and kisses her fingers one by one.

It hurts. Everything in my body hurts.

Dee Shhh.

Jamie I want it to stop.

Dee You want to leave this room?

Jamie Not any more.

Dee You sure?

Jamie Every day you ask me. I'm sure. (*Beat.*) So cold in here.

Dee It's spring outside.

Jamie Is it?

Dee Maybe.

Jamie Say it again.

Dee Maybe. Maybe.

Jamie I'm getting spoiled.

Dee Maybe.

Young Jamie and Young Dee are suddenly with them now. The two realities happen simultaneously. Young Dee is ready to leave and carries a small bag of belongings.

Young Jamie You're not supposed to be here.

Young Dee Peppermints. Gave a handful to that new guard, Grinder, the one with no teeth. He says I got ten minutes to say goodbye.

Young Jamie Goodbye, Dee.

Jamie You could change your mind. You could go.

Dee I'm where I want to go.

Young Dee It's only a few years.

Jamie Let me see it now. I'm ready.

Young Jamie If we stay away from trouble, we'll both be out at the same time.

Young Dee You got the address memorised?

Dee pulls an elegant knife from beneath the mattress. She holds it up for Jamie to see. They both stare at the knife between them.

Young Jamie 149 West Madison 16B. Just round the corner from BB-Jigs hardware.

Jamie Only thing we ever stole from them classy homes.

Dee I stole it.

Jamie But I told you to.

Young Dee I'll fix it up 'fore you get there. It will be our place.

Young Jamie Our place.

Young Dee I'll check the Want ads. Find out where they're needing work.

Young Jamie But only the best. 'Cause we trained all this time.

Young Dee Only the best.

Jamie touches the knife's blade.

Jamie There's a spilling inside me.

Dee Yeah.

Young Jamie Don't forget what we learned. It's gonna keep us kickin' when we get out.

Young Dee I won't forget a thing.

Jamie Like a pinprick inside me. A hole. And I'm pouring down that hole.

Dee Do me first, Jamie.

Young Jamie I'm glad you came here.

Dee That's what we agreed.

Young Jamie That first time. Months back.

Dee 'Cause I'm a coward. I might change my mind.

Young Dee You almost hit me.

Jamie You're not a coward.

Dee Yeah, I am. With big teeth.

Young Jamie Course I almost hit you. Barging in like that.

Jamie Dee.

Dee First time I saw you walking in the prison yard I thought –

Young Jamie Crazy girl. Shows up in my cell, what was I to do?

Dee
– There goes a piece of morning.

Young Dee Like being born when we get out.

Dee
There goes the break of day.
If I could snatch her attention,
She'd never go away.

Young Dee We can make this work.

Jamie And I thought –

Young Jamie I'll wait for you.

Jamie
  – There goes the still of water.
  There goes the spill of night.

Young Dee And I'll wait for you. I swear it.

Jamie
  If I turn my back on her . . . peppermints,
  I'll never make it right.

Dee Dumber than me!

Young Dee We're gonna do this side by side.

Jamie Come here.

Young Jamie Side by side.

Jamie Stand close to me.

  Dee steps closer to Jamie.

Close.

Young Jamie Feels like my head will bust.

Dee I'm not sorry, Jamie. About anything.

Young Jamie That's how happy I am.

  *Jamie abruptly stabs Dee in the stomach. At the same
  time Young Dee lets out a wild, loud celebratory call.
  Dee doubles over, holding her stomach. Jamie stands
  still, holding the knife at her side.*

Young Dee I am ready!

Jamie Stand up straight.

Dee I can't.

Jamie Yes, you can.

Dee straightens up. Jamie and Dee are face to face, not quite touching.

Young Jamie Well. Say goodbye.

Young Dee I don't want to.

Jamie If this is what it is.

Dee Yeah.

Jamie Here with you.

Young Jamie Goodbye, Dee.

Jamie Then I don't mind.

Jamie takes Dee's hand and puts the knife in it but holds on to Dee's hand.

Young Dee Let's just shake hands.

Jamie I want to undress you again.

Young Jamie All right.

Dee I want you to undress me again.

Jamie Make you call for me.

Young Dee Jamie.

Dee (*whispers to her*) Jamie.

Jamie, with Dee helping, pushes the knife into her own stomach. Dee moves away, dropping the knife, and kneels. Jamie still stands.

Young Jamie Don't forget.

Jamie (*almost surprised*) It hurts.

Young Jamie All new. It's gonna be all new.

The young women remain standing.

Young Dee I promise you that.

Young Jamie I can feel a heat in my chest. That's a promise too.

Young Dee I can feel that heat. If I gave you a cup of water it'd boil in your hand.

Young Jamie (*laughs*) That's freedom's heat –

Dee I'm happy, Jamie.

Young Jamie – and it's just round the corner.

Jamie So am I.

Jamie comes to kneel beside Dee. The women are both calm, as though at the centre of a storm.

Young Dee Two rags, two buckets.

Young Jamie And lots of water.

Jamie Hush. I hear it.

Dee What?

Jamie It's coming for us.

Young Jamie That's all we'll need.

Young Dee You swear when we meet up, you'll stay with me?

Dee I'm scared.

Jamie Be quiet. It's all right now.

Young Dee Promise you'll stay with me.

Jamie Its all right. Hush.

Young Jamie Yes. I promise. I promise, now hush.

Young Jamie / Jamie Hush.

Young Jamie / Young Dee / Jamie / Dee Hush.

End of play.